see (MC—)2 boy 1st on tape
raised by goth mother & learned to
do self hypnosis by health reading
by visualization
— now says
its demonic
Power.

HYPNOTISM
Divine
or
DEMONIC

By
LESTER SUMRALL

Enlarged & Revised
1988

17   Hypnotism is very bad.

Unless otherwise indicated,
all Scripture quotations are taken from
the *King James Version* of the Bible.

Hypnotism
ISBN 0-937580-05-8
Copyright © 1988 by
Lester Sumrall Evangelistic Association
Published by LESEA Publishing Company
P.O. Box 12
South Bend, Indiana 46624

Contents

1

THE HYPNOSIS INVASION

THE IMMENSE power and growing popularity of hypnotism coupled with the gross ignorance of the general public concerning the real issues involved demand that this book be written NOW.

With all the subtlety and sinuous intrigue at hell's command, the unsuspecting man in the street is being bombarded with the dubious claims of hypnotism. Brightly colored, cross-my-palm-with-silver leaflets extolling the prowess of this or that professor of hypnotism dropped unasked into our mail boxes. Television and the popular press are lending hypnotism an aura of respectability by featuring the demonstrations, lectures and writings of a host of exponents. Bizarre ads appear frequently in a variety of occult-slanted magazines calculated to raise the goose-pimples of the dabblers in the unknown.

HYPNOSIS MOVES INTO SOCIETY

No longer is hypnotism limited to the vaudeville stage or the seamy sideshows of the county fair. The attraction is deeper now than just a few shyster stunts with a pretty stooge in a scanty costume. Hypnotism is now high society. An exclusive dinner or cocktail party is hardly complete nowadays without the performance of a hypnotist or psychic showman. Following the current do-it-yourself trend, people are foolishly practicing home-hypnotism as family entertainment.

Even more puzzling is the increased

influence of this so-called science in the realms of medicine, education and religion. Doctors, educators and ministers are succumbing in dangerous numbers to the siren song of hypnotism as the key to the subconscious, the locked inner-man—the soul of man. The contamination of psychic phenomena is spreading through our land like the spores of some self-proliferating fungus. The people must know the dangers involved. Hypnotism is a poisonous art. It is not an innocent, harmless party frolic. It is an explosive, destructive and contagious menace.

BAPTIST PASTOR A HYPNOTIST

A Baptist pastor from Chicago visited our church in South Bend and told the following story.

He discovered when he was a child 9 or 10 years old that he could hypnotize other children. He began to study hypnotism from any books or magazines he could lay hands on.

When in Jr. High and High School, it was soon discovered that he could hypnotize and he was invited to all the parties. When even the teacher could be hypnotized, he was the "lion" of the party.

In Moody Bible Institute he carried his hypnotism further and again was invited to all school parties and asked to hypnotize.

Then, in the Northern Baptist Seminary he further did hypnotism at their parties.

After graduation and taking a Baptist church, he met a Christian who invited him to breakfast. He discovered it was a Full Gospel Businessmen's breakfast.

After breakfast, one of the laymen at his table leaned very closely and said, "Sir, excuse me, but you have two devils in you."

The Baptist pastor said he was enraged and told him, "If you are so smart, tell me what they are."

The Christian businessman was humbled and said, "It is not me, but the Holy Spirit revealing your condition. The first demon is a spirit of hypnotism."

The Baptist pastor said he was amazed because they were strangers, but he spoke back and said, "I may have one devil, but I do not have two. What is the other one?"

The Christian layman responded, "It is a spirit of denominationalism. You want everybody to be a Baptist."

By this time the pastor was humbled and said, "Will you please cast them out?" The layman prayed for him and he felt instant relief and now praises God that he has been set free.

2

THE HISTORY OF HYPNOSIS

IF we are to properly understand hypnotism, we must **study its origins.** To appreciate its association in the lives of modern people, we must also observe **who has used it** through the centuries and why. We will then come to know the true implications of this black art.

MEET HYPNOS, A GREEK GOD
Our word, hypnotism, comes to us from a Greek word, *hypnos,* which means "sleep."

Hypnos was the winged god of Greek mythology. The Romans called him Somnus, the god of sleep. According to Greek legend, he was the son of Erebus (the son of Chaos) and Nox, the goddess of night.

The Roman version of Hypnos' story (Somnus, as they called him) was that he lived in a massive cave with his brother, the god of death. Outside flowed the River of Forgetfulness, one drink of which was reputed to erase all memories. Inside the cave the light was dim and everything slept. Pleasant dreams and dark nightmares flitted to and fro like cheesecloth at a seance. So much for the Hypnos family!

HYPNOSIS
THE SLEEPING DECEPTION

Hypnosis, then, has long been held out as a delightful condition of forgetfulness, allied to the careless sleep of death where there are no worries or retributions. Practically from the beginning of time, it seems, men have turned to hypnosis as an escape mechanism from the pressures of life. It has seemed to many as inviting as suicide, without the complete finality of death.

Enlightened scientists, on the other hand, consider hypnosis to be controversial and warn that hypnotism by unqualified persons is dangerous. (To which we add; Hypnotism by ALL kinds of persons is dangerous!) Medical doctors know that hypnosis brings a change in a person's conscious awareness. The consciousness narrows, much as it does during a dream or a vision. However, the hypnotized person is different from a sleeping person, in that he is active. He can walk, talk or write. He may remain quiet, but in most cases will obey suggestions by the hypnotist in performing actions.

In other words, a hypnotized person is in a state of abnormal concentration, induced by an operator. (This description could be used with equal force to explain the condition of a demon-possessed individual.)

There is a strong hint of hypnotism

in the very mists of time. Back in the Garden of Eden, is it not feasible that the Serpent hypnotized Eve, even as a snake petrifies a rabbit with its piercing gaze and magnetic rhythm? Lucifer, master of all fallen wisdom, the hypnotist, whispered the illegal suggestion to Mother Eve. Gripping her mind through his devilish eyes, did he induce that state of unconcern which made her forget God's command?

We know he lied to her. "Ye shall be as gods. God doesn't want you to eat of this tree because He doesn't want you to be like Him. He's holding information back from you!" Eve, paying heed to the seducer's voice, did what he suggested—and sin entered into the world!

MESMERISM

In the latter part of the 18th century, Franz A. Mesmer, a Viennese physician, introduced the practice of hypnotism (it became known as Mesmerism) into the scientific world. He described it as an occult force, which he called "animal magnetism." Modern science seeks to discredit Mesmer's belief that hypnosis is in the sphere of the supernatural. He had, however, more understanding of the forces that the hypnotist unleashes than his modern counterparts imagine. In the middle of the 19th century, James Braid, an English physician, gave hypnotism its modern name.

BODY, SOUL, SPIRIT

Today there is a strong renaissance of the practice of hypnotism. Let us see how this has come about.

For centuries man was an earth-bound creature. He could not travel any faster than a horse could carry him. He was truly an earthman, tied to the earth.

Later, as he developed the craft of boat-building, man took to the great waterways and began to sail the seven seas in mighty boats. Man had broken out of his landlocked dimension. Now he could visit the continents in voyages of discovery.

In our century, man broke forth into yet another dimension of travel. He began to fly like a bird. From walking upright on the land, he learned to swim like a fish, and now he moves through the air like a bird. Man has moved into his last dimension in this world: from the earth, to the water, to the air.

These three parallel the trinity of man: walking on the land speaks of the body, the flesh; moving through the water tallies with the soul; and flying through the air is the realm of the spirit. We are now living in the Age of the Spirit, or the Last Times. The battle, then, of the Last Times will be a battle of the Spirit.

The devil is clearly operating in the realm of the spirit of man in these days. There are many symptoms of this. Spiritism as a religion is growing faster in popularity than any other form of religion known to man right now. Men are giving themselves over to spirits. Occultism, mysticism, black magic, these things are enticing the hungry hearts of men. With them has come this latter-day resurgence of hypnotism.

THE BLACK ART

At this point, let me go on record with a categorical and uncompromising statement: Hypnotism is a black art. It is bad, always bad, never good, but absolutely bad, completely bad, wholly bad!

How can I be so emphatic? Control of your mind and your will-power is the greatest God-given privilege you have. Anyone who robs you of this privilege is a thief. Jesus says that the devil is a thief and a robber, and he comes only to kill and to steal and to destroy.

Anytime anyone takes your mind from you, they are taking the greatest thing you have. Without your mind you cannot find God. I have never heard of insane people finding God. Without your mind you do not know the way home, you do not know how to work, you know nothing.

PROTECT YOUR TREASURE

Your mind is your treasure to hold. Why would you give it to somebody else? Why would you let a man take your mind out of your control, so that he can totally command what you are to do? I do not know if you have let yourself be hypnotized. What I do know is that if you have, your soul was and still may be in great danger.

If you were to offer me $100,000, I would not let any human hypnotize me for even two minutes. You say, "Why?" Well, once another has taken over your mind and you do not have control of it, you have opened yourself up to the total spirit world. The Bible tells us that the devil is the prince of the power of the air. Under hypnosis, you have opened the door to him. The operator who brings you into a trance cannot protect you from the works of the devil. No human being can take care of you once you yield yourself in this way to the spirit world. I do not care how much power and control the operator thinks he has, the devil is a lot bigger than he is, and he is playing in the devil's territory.

What about the operator, the hypnotist? Is he safe? Is he immune from evil influence? No, sir! He has to open himself up to strange powers in order to gain control over another's mind. The moment you enter the devil's territory to operate on his lines you are open to every evil force he cares to send along. Do not try to practice hypnotism on anyone. You will be opening your soul for the devil to possess you!

3

THE POWER OF HYPNOTISM

HYPNOTISM is a phenomenon which possesses power either to curb or create pain. It can produce reality or unreality. It has power. *Look Magazine,* in an article by Ralph Diagh, said, "Before a group of doctors at a medical convention in Atlantic City, New Jersey, a hypnotized doctor was told that he would be touched on the forearm with a red hot iron and that a blister would form as a result. The hypnotist touched the doctor on the arm with an ordinary wooden pencil. The doctor jerked his arm away in obvious pain, and a blister formed, as if he had actually been burned by an iron."

Joan Brondon, the operator who hypnotized the physician said, "A person under hypnosis is extremely susceptible to suggestion from the hypnotist. Any suggestion I give the subject, with very few exceptions, is accepted by him as reality."

UNCANNY POWERS OF HYPNOSIS

The unnatural suggestibility induced by hypnosis can cause the subject to become deaf, dumb, blind, hallucinatory, disoriented, or anesthetized.

Under hypnosis, the average person can do amazing feats not possible in the conscious state. A hypnotized man might quite easily multiply 267 by 3892 in his head by mental arithmetic in a matter of seconds. A subject's memory may be jogged to where he can recite verbatim the first page of his first school reader. The mental aspects of hypnotism are what fascinate modern educators, who are toying with its use as a teaching medium.

One of the mysteries of hypnosis is the subject's amazing ability to estimate posthypnotic time with baffling accuracy. One subject was told under a trance that he would ring a bell six hours after being awakened. Brought to himself in a completely darkened and windowless room, he was introduced to the bell and told to remain where he was. Six hours and two minutes later, without contact with the outside world, he rang the bell!

It has been said that no subject can be induced to do anything contrary to his own moral principles. However, scientists have proved that hypnotized persons can and will perform antisocial and even self-distructive acts. To achieve this, the operator must deceive the subject. For example, under hypnosis a normally modest woman would refuse point-blank to remove her clothes if the suggestion were made directly. However, if the operator suggested that she was in the seclusion of her own bathroom, for example, she might well disrobe before the whole audience. The subject, then, is at the mercy of the operator to a greater degree than any one person should permit himself to be influenced by another person!

How does a hypnotist succeed in getting a subject to surrender his will? First, he must get the subject relaxed. He then perhaps instructs the subject to close his eyes and to breathe deeply. When the subject is concentrating properly and has accepted these suggestions, he is given the final suggestions: "You are sleepy; you are going to sleep; you are asleep." The subject is then in a hypnotic trance.

No person can be hypnotized against his will. Hypnosis may be avoided simply by refusing attention to the hypnotist's words, or by deliberately thinking of something else, like reciting the multiplication table or mentally humming a tune.

Science, however, is not willing to leave things there. Research is under way to investigate techniques that will allow persons to be hypnotized without their knowledge, desire or consent. Drugs like sodium pentothal (the "truth serum") and certain barbiturates are already in use to break down a subject's resistance to hypnosis.

During hypnosis a subject is open to two kinds of suggestions: hypnotic and posthypnotic. The hypnotic suggestions he will perform there and then. They may include hallucination, in which he will see, hear, or feel things that are not actually present. He can be induced to feel imaginary ants crawling on his skin, and may go frantic trying to brush them off.

Catalepsy, a state of muscle rigidity, can be induced as a hypnotic suggestion. This is a popular trick of stage magicians, who will suspend a stiffened subject head-and-heel between two chairs like a board. Doctors have used this technique to keep patients in one position for long periods of time, especially when intricate skin graftings are involved. A person has been known to hold his arm fast in one position for several weeks under hypnosis, with no discomfort.

Age regression, the taking of the subject back in time, too, is the result of hypnotic suggestion. By this means psychiatrists endeavor to have patients relive the traumatic experiences of their childhood.

Unfortunately, quite often, if the operator fails to release the person completely from the age regression suggestion, they come out of the trance with worse neuroses than when they went under.

A similar danger is present with the cataleptic condition induced by hypnotism. Here again, a subject could find himself with an unresponsive stiff limb after the trance, due to the failure of the operator to remove the suggestion entirely. There have been victims with posthypnotic damage after the well-publicized visits of some vaudeville hypnotists. It's a dangerous business!

Although there is normally no rememberance by the subject of what took place under the hypnotic trance, there is the remarkable phenomenon of posthypnotic behavior as a result of suggestions given by the hypnotist while the subject was under hypnosis. We have already spoken of the man who was able to ring a bell accurately on time six hours after the posthypnotic suggestion was made. By this means, the operator can control the future actions of a subject, even though separated by distance.

It may well be that the plot of the remarkable book, *The Manchurian Candidate,* may not be too farfetched. Through communist brainwashing and hypnosis an American G.I. prisoner-of-war was conditioned to answer to a posthypnotic suggestion and to kill on command. He was conditioned to obey the first instruction given him after seeing a certain playing card. This card triggered the posthypnotic reflex in him. The aim was to have him assassinate the presidential candidate.

THE POWER OF THE HYPNOSIS OPERATOR

Apart from the fact, then, that

hypnotism opens up the soul of a man to the works of the devil, it also puts him under the control of men who may be evil in themselves. Under hypnosis a person is unable to carry out his own desires or fully maintain his own moral standards. His reasoning processes are rendered helpless. He will believe anything the operator tells him. So far as exercising his own will is concerned, he is no better off than a zombie while in a trance.

Whatever the power of hypnotism is, then, its results are very real. It is obvious that science is still groping for its true meaning, and that, despite the alluring "benefits" it seems to offer, the dangers are far greater, the consequences far graver, and, as the Bible says so plainly: the wages of sin are death! There is no doubt in my mind that tapping the power-source of hypnotism is in direct conflict with God's wishes. *Regard not them that have familiar spirits, neither seek after wizards, to be defiled by them: I am the LORD your God* (Leviticus 19:31).

4

EDUCATION AND HYPNOTISM

WHO is leading this revival of hypnotism?

To a large degree, it is being promoted by apparently respectable psychiatrists, physicians, dentists, educators and religious leaders. Whole masses of people swallow the cult of hypnotism without a moment's hesitation, merely because it is given a seeming "seal of safety" by these learned gentlemen.

TEACHERS PRACTICE
HYPNOSIS ON STUDENTS

These men all practice their professions; and in the case of hypnosis, "practice" is the operative word. Delving into the unknown and probably unknowable recesses of the human mind, even the best-intentioned practitioner is only experimenting. The patient or subject is nothing more than a human guinea pig. Nobody knows for certain what the outcome of the treatment will be. The external signs may seem favorable after hypnosis, but the damage done to the soul of the man and the subtle derangements of his inner emotions, are incalculable. Herein lies the danger of hypnotism!

Perhaps the most frightening aspect of hypnotic practice is in the field of education. Prone as they are to demonic attack in any case, what kind of warping and twisting could be done to the mind of an innocent, un-molded child through suggestions? Would you be content to have your child at the mercy of some teacher/hypnotist, manipulating the youngster's mind like pliant clay? Yet I have in my possession a news clipping which tells of an Italian professor in a boys' school who took a group of pupils and hypnotized every one of them. He gave them a lecture and read them a long poem. When he broke the power of the trance, each boy was able to repeat the poem word for word, although they had only heard it once in their lives! The fact which most captured the professor's imagination was that, after the trance, the dull boys were as bright concerning that lecture and poem as the bright boys.

You can see the awful temptation here for educators to take a short cut through the normal rough-and-tumble method of imparting knowledge to a group of average or below average students, by turning to hypnotism. It is the rough-and-tumble feeding and exercising of young minds that is the very process of education.

THE ROLE OF THE HOLY SPIRIT

The powerful forces of good which these men are seeking to release and harness within the heart of other men through hypnotism, are only genuinely released through the workings of the Holy Spirit. Every worthwhile thing hypnotism seeks, and usually fails to accomplish, can be accomplished through prayer. Let a man be born again of the Spirit of God, through faith in our Lord Jesus Christ. Let him be baptized by the Holy Spirit and be empowered from on high. Let him pray the prayer of faith, and he will accomplish wonders undreamed of in the shaky realm of hypnotism.

Remember the words of Jesus, when He said, *But the Comforter, which is the Holy Ghost, whom the Father will send in my name, he shall teach you all things, and bring all things to your remembrance. . .he will guide you into all truth: for he shall not speak of himself; but whatsoever he shall hear, that shall he speak: and he will show you things to come* (John 14:26; 16:13).

If Christian parents would teach their children to believe those promises and look to God for help in their

studies, there would be fewer class-
room breakdowns and a lot better
grades. I know of one girl, the
daughter of missionary parents, who
has been to over twelve different
schools in five different countries. She
is not exceptionally gifted nor
remarkably intelligent, yet because
she has been taught by her parents to
approach each school day depending
on the Lord, she has been a consistent
honor roll student in each school.

5

HYPNOSIS AS THERAPY

A PROMINENT publisher of scholarly treatises says, "Hypnotism is widely accepted today at its proper level—as a legitimate field of scientific inquiry and a useful tool of psychotherapy. Its potential has been recognized by the British Medical Society and the American Medical Association, and courses on the subject are appearing in medical schools and in training programs for psychiatrists. Many psychologists, too, have turned to hypnosis as a fertile field for research and therapy. This widespread interest dates only from the Second

World War. Previously hypnosis had a checkered career over a period of centuries, going through cycle after cycle of general approval and then total eclipse.

In one of these cycles, pioneer doctors performed surgery on hypnotized patients, successfully using hypnosis as an anesthetic; but the medical societies insisted the patients were only pretending not to feel pain! Before that issue was settled, chloroform and other chemical anesthetics were developed, and interest in hypnotism died.

Of course, for Christians, there is no "proper level" nor "legitimate field" so far as hypnotism is concerned. As for having recognized its potential, the doctors of the BMS and the AMA ought to know that in spite of superficial "benefits" whose worth has never yet been fully assessed, the potential of hypnotism is evil.

Out of all the publisher's misconceptions and misstatements, there remains one clarion fact: hypnotism is being widely accepted today in the medical world.

HYPNOSIS IS NOT THERAPY

Actually, the most common use for hypnosis by medical doctors is not strictly therapeutic, that is for the healing of disease. It is as an anesthetic. Patients have been hypnotized for childbirth, for dental surgery, during the setting of a fracture, and for other types of surgery. In a deep trance a patient is supposed to lose all feeling and become immune to pain. However, this can only be as a result of causing some part of the brain to cease to function correctly. The cause of the pain still remains. The patient ought to feel pain. If he does not, it is because his brain has been forced to quit interpreting the information the cut or diseased nerve ends are sending to it. This is a dangerous mental condition to be in. A hypnotist, using the anesthetic property of hypnotism, might easily remove the consciousness of a man to pain so that the pain symptoms of his illness cease. The patient might think he is cured, when in fact, the disease could be ravaging his body unchecked, without the danger signals of pain which are intended to warn him that his body is being attacked. Unless his sickness also has some external, visible signs to alert him, he might imagine that he is healed—and die in his deception.

THE DECEIVER

Hypnosis is a deceiver. The devil is a deceiver. You can tell they belong together. Hypnosis doesn't cure anything. It just makes you think something doesn't exist.

The AMA has some strong words to say about symptom removal through hypnosis. It is very definitely dangerous, "particularly when the focus of the treatment is on the symptom rather than the underlying cause of the symptom."

They go on to tell how a woman chain smoker was treated by a hypnotist. She quit smoking, but became a compulsive eater and gained 40 pounds! She went to another hypnotist who "cured" the overeating problem. She became an alcoholic instead! If she had tried one more hypnotic "cure" she might have slipped from alcoholism to drug addiction or even suicide!

Another sufferer had a severe back pain caused by what psychiatrists call "depressive equivalent." In other words, the pain was only a substitute for an underlying depression. A hypno-therapist quickly cured the back pain, but the patient's depression then took over and he committed suicide!

Hypno-therapeutics in the field of psychiatry is a subject too complex and confusing to deal with here in detail. The more one looks at psychiatry the more one is inclined to think that half the psychiatrists themselves are not sure what they are up to. It is almost a case of every man for himself, and the devil take the hindmost.

We have already touched upon age regression, or the taking of the subject back into childhood. Here again, no-one can be certain how much of what is remembered under hypnosis is reality, how much is fantasy, or how much is merely the result of insinuations and suggestions made by the probing psychiatrist. An overeager operator can easily implant his own ideas and interpretations into a subject, so that the patient not only has his own problems, but may end up with some of the hypnotist's too!

The hypno-psychiatrist uses suggestion in a variety of ways to unlock a patient's troubled mind, remove a mental block, or alleviate his psychosis or madness in some way. This whole so-called science is so inexact that no-one can anticipate the end result of such hypnotic sessions.

AUTOHYPNOSIS

Autohypnosis, or hypnotizing oneself, is also easily performed. The AMA warns, "can however be dangerous to the person using it." It has been used successfully for the relief of pain, but those who use it have a tendency to withdraw from the world of reality. They use autohypnosis as an escape mechanism. Many, say the AMA, have brought on psychoses (mental disorders) through self-hypnosis. "Careful study by a physician trained in the dynamics of hypnosis is essential before allowing self-hypnosis." But what man understands the dynamics or the power structure of hypnosis? Like electricity, technicians have a fair idea what it does, but no one really knows what it is.

It is clear that autohypnosis leads to temporary demon possession. The Balinese of Indonesia practice it extensively in their traditional rituals. How else can one explain the self-induced trance of the demon-cult priestesses of Brazil and Dahomey, W. Africa, who become possessed by frenzied demons as part of their religion, than that this is self-hypnosis?

Make no mistake: this self-hypnosis is only to bring on the trance. Once the demons take over there is no question of hallucination or imagination. The devil's presence is REAL!

Are the frenzied dances of the fetish princesses any more devilish than the possession which takes place in an American spiritist medium at a "respectable" seance? The same process of self-induced trance followed by the taking over of the vocal chords of the medium is in evidence. Is this not, then, autohypnosis at its worst? Are you still in doubt about whether the devil wants to take over your life if only you will let him? If you hypnotize yourself or let someone else do it for you, the devil will step in!

A significant statement from an eminent practitioner of hypnotherapy, Dr. Hippolyte Bernheim, (although not intended by him as a warning), should be sufficient to reveal the dangers involved here: "Sometimes the subject resists. We have noticed that even in hypnotic sleep his will is not always destroyed." This, then, is the basis of hypnotic suggestion: the destruction of another human being's will. Can you think of a more ungodly undertaking? As the American Medical Association says, "It is important to point out that dangerous complications can result from the indiscriminate use of hypnosis." I believe this to be a true statement.

THE ONLY TRUE HEALER

If a man needs healing in his spirit, in his mind, or in his body, let him come to God, Who says, "I am the Lord that healeth thee." God does not demand that a man become an automaton, a mental cripple, a creature without a will of his own, in order to cure him. Hypnotism, with all its gaudy promises, demands just that—and cannot guarantee a cure at all!

Let me say it again: there is no place in a decent, God-fearing society for the practice of hypnotism, even disguised in the cap and gown of a doctor of degree.

6

SOCIETY & HYPNOTISM

THE AURA of respectability which professional men are giving to hypnotism is fast winning it a place in the warp and woof of our modern society. Even the legal profession is being tempted to make use of hypnosis as a medium for arriving at evidential truth. There seems to be a mistaken theory that hypnotism can be used like a lie-detector or truth serum.

THE HYPNOSIS WITNESS

A close study of Dr. H. Bernheim's classic textbook on the subject, *Hypnosis and Suggestion*, should disillusion anyone.

Bernheim tells how he set up a susceptible young man by suggestion, until the patient was ready to swear in court to what he had "witnessed."

Charles R., an Italian mason, twenty years old, was in the hospital for tubercular pleurisy. He had no nervous history, but Bernheim discovered he was very open to hypnotic suggestion. The doctor asked Charles if he had witnessed a fight between two drunken male nurses, during which one had his leg broken. The young man responded that he wasn't present and did not know.

The operator then made the strong suggestion: "You told me about it this morning. . ." and went on to describe the details. Bernheim goes on record: "In about two minutes the hallucinatory memory had dawned on his mind. He saw it." The subject went on to describe in great detail the incident he had never seen.

"I asked him for the man's name, in order to give it to the police commissioner," writes Bernheim. "He should tell what he had seen and should take his oath."

Telling the subjects that they were mistaken only made them angry. The subjects persisted in believing the false evidence because they saw a retroactive hallucination that had been created.

PROFESSIONAL LIARS

If society accepts hypnotism into our law courts after testimony like this, we are headed for chaos (called after Hypnos' grandfather, remember Ch. 1)! Listen to the learned doctor once more: "Some subjects relate the facts with surprising accuracy of detail. Like a professional liar, they invent out of whole cloth, with imperturbable coolness and perfect conviction. Their imagination suggests all the circumstances of the self-conceived drama."

The Lord Jesus Christ said that Satan is the father of all lies. What kind of devilish web do men weave when they first start out to deceive the passive subjects of their hypnotic arts? Anything that will get a man's mind into the state where he cannot tell truth from falsehood, reality from unreality, fact from fantasy, is a work of the devil. Paul, writing to the Ephesians, nails it fair and square: *And have no fellowship with the unfruitful works of darkness, but rather reprove them* (Ephesians 5:11).

7

THE CHURCH
AND HYPNOTISM

WHEN the Church of Jesus Christ
was a power in the world and
when the Church had something to
say about the way nations lived, there
was very little hypnotism in Christian
lands. It was banned and banished
and fought as a tool of the devil. The
Early Christians condemned hypnosis.
They believed that the subjects came
under the power of the devil.

THE POWERLESS CHURCH
Today the Church has lost its author-
ity. Neither men nor governments pay

heed to its word any more. Hypnotism rides through the land unchallenged, like a dark horseman, deceiving people in every walk of life.

Buy the average magazine, and you will find a dozen places to write for lessons on how to become a hypnotist. Ordinary people are being urged to meddle with the delicate balance of the minds of their friends and families, all in the name of "FUN." Christian, you had better have nothing to do with this kind of fun if you do not want to damn your friends into the devil's clutches.

GOD'S WORD WARNS ABOUT HYPNOSIS

The Church ought to speak out on hypnotism. It ought to have an opinion. Not the opinions of churchmen, but God's opinion spoken through His Church. What the world needs to hear from the Church is not a committee report, but a message from Heaven. We need the oracles of God, not the offscouring of modern man's intellect.

WORSHIPING THE FIRE GOD

Deuteronomy 18:10, *There shall not*

be found among you any one that maketh his son or his daughter to pass through the fire. . .

This forbidden practice was a heathen ritual to demonstrate superiority over fire, and to prove that they were immune to flames. There are still fire walkers in India, Malaysia, Indonesia and Africa. They put themselves into a trance, probably by autohypnosis, and become oblivious to pain in a very strange way.

God forbade His people to do this. He would not tolerate it or permit it at all!

DIVINATION

Then verse 10 goes on, *or that useth divination. . .*"divination" is foretelling the future by other than human means. A diviner is one who can tell things that are going to happen by a power other than human reasoning. This form of spiritism is practiced among heathen people extensively. It is becoming widespread in America, too. Even Christian people are being tempted to delve into the unlawful seeking after knowledge of the future.

Crystal balls, palm reading, horoscopes, reading the cards, fortune telling, ESP (extra-sensory perception), these are the rib-ticklers some people are turning to for assurance, for comfort, for entertainment. God says that you must not do it. Do not go to fortune tellers for spiritual, material or any kind of advice. That is a good way to get a curse upon your life.

I have had people tell me that they began to play with a Ouija board just for a thrill or just to unlock a few secrets. To their sorrow they discovered that the "harmless" Ouija board had gotten hold of them, and they could not turn it loose. As if drawn by some unseen power, again and again they were pulled back to another session with the spooky board. They had become spiritual slaves!

You can go to gypsies and fortune tellers seeking guidance until you become so entangled with it that you will be scared to make a decision without first consulting the spirit. You will be the pawn of a familiar spirit who can tell you just about anything and you will believe it! God says this should not be practiced among His people.

OBSERVING TIMES

Then God adds, *or an observer of the times. . .* An observer of the times is one who watches the stars and tries to tell what is going to happen by astrology. These are the kind who read your horoscope. Hitler was completely dominated by the advice of one of these stargazers. Some of the worst blunders he ever made during World War II were as a result of the wicked advice this man gave him. God says it is not harmless fun. It is black magic. God knows you can become addicted to this kind of thing just as you can to drugs. You can be deceived completely. That is the work of the devil. God will not allow this kind of thing in His family.

ENCHANTERS

God then says, *or an enchanter. . .* This is one who practices the secret arts, charming serpents, casting demonic spells over other people. These are the kind who stick pins in dolls to bring on pains in the person to be enchanted. What difference is there between that kind of enchanter and a hypnotic operator who casts a spell over his subject. You say, "Would you call hypnotism casting a spell?" I reply, "What else would you call it?"

FAMILIAR SPIRITS

Verse 10 finishes and goes into verse 11, *or a witch, or a charmer, or a consulter with familiar spirits, or a wizard, or a necromancer.* That just about covers the whole putrefying bunch, doesn't it?

God further declares in verse 12, *For all that do these things are an abomination unto the LORD: and because of these abominations the LORD thy God doth drive them out from before thee.*

In case anyone is still in doubt about God's opinion, let me quote from the New Testament, from Paul's letter to the Ephesians, chapter 5, verses 6 through 14,

Let no man deceive you with vain words: for because of these things

cometh the wrath of God upon the children of disobedience. Be ye not therefore partakers with them. For ye were sometimes darkness, but now ye are light in the Lord: walk as children of light: (For the fruit of the Spirit is in all goodness and righteousness and truth;) proving what is acceptable unto the Lord.

And have no fellowship with the unfruitful works of darkness, but rather reprove them. For it is a shame even to speak of those things which are done of them in secret. But all things that are reproved are made manifest by the light: for whatsoever doth make manifest is light.

Wherefore he saith, Awake thou that sleepest, and arise from the dead, and Christ shall give thee light.

HYPNOTISM AND THE END OF THE WORLD

HYPNOTISM has a clearly prophetic relationship to the end of the world. In fact, to understand the present phenomenal surge of hypnotism, it must be studied dispensationally.

In Matthew 24, the Lord Jesus specifically said to His disciples, *Let no one deceive you.* This was His first response to the question asked about His coming again to this earth and the end of the world. Hypnosis is a condition of deception. Hypnotism has no divine life that can make a man better, or cleaner or happier. All it can do is open the soul's door to demon invasion.

KING SAUL'S DOWNFALL

God firmly established His attitude toward this spiritual phenomenon. In I Chronicles 10:13-14 we read, *So Saul died for his transgression which he committed against the LORD, even against the word of the LORD, which he kept not, and also for asking counsel of one that had a familiar spirit, to inquire of it; and inquired not of the LORD. . .*

Israel's first king was rejected, and died at his own hand, to be eternally lost, for the simple reason that he took counsel of a familiar spirit. It was a grave offense against God. Our minds are sacred. We must not open them up to any other power than the power of God.

SEDUCING SPIRITS

In I Timothy 4:1 the Apostle Paul said, *Now the Spirit speaketh expressly, that in the latter times some shall de-*

*part from the faith, giving heed to se-
ducing spirits, and doctrines of devils.*
Every intelligent person realizes that
we are nearing the end of something.
At this time, the thinking men of our
generation sense something of the at-
mosphere which existed in Babylon
the night the empire was dissolved
and the finger of God wrote Belshaz-
zar's doom upon the wall, . . .*Thou art
weighed in the balances and found
wanting.*   (Daniel 5:27)

Our modern world ought to feel the
rumblings in the foundations of
civilization that were felt in the Roman
Empire when 40% of the nation's in-
come was squandered on public
orgies of blood in the circus arenas. As
the hungry flames broke out to con-
sume the haughty world capital, Rome
crumbled and fell through her own
licentiousness.

It ought to shock us to realize that
our generation is also spending
millions of dollars seeking thrills and
"truth" from soothsayers, fortune
tellers, crystal-gazers, clairvoyants,
hypnotists and mediums. In our social

life we are spending millions of dollars
for such trash as Ouija boards and
Tarot cards and anything that promises to tell us the future. In the up-
per echelons of society, prognos-
ticators like Jeane Dixon mingle with
great ease, even catching the ears of
our politicians and administrators
with their lying vanities.

America is on the brink of the pit of
disaster into which the nation Israel
fell when King Saul consulted a witch
for advice.

When man refuses to hear or obey
the voice of God, inevitably he is
forced to seek some other voice to
guide him. That other voice is the
voice of the devil!

THE ANTICHRIST

In Revelation, chapter 13, the Bible
says that the Antichrist will suffer a
deadly wound and be miraculously
healed. Then he will show himself to
be a wonder to the world. His religious
leader, known as the False Prophet,
will cause a statue to speak and the
people to bow down to it. He will even

cause fire to come down from heaven in the sight of men.

This will be the greatest battle of all time. The devil will be seeking with every means in his power to conquer the mind, soul and spirit of mankind. The last great battle on this earth is to be a battle for the spirit and mind of man.

Your mind must not be clouded by fear and phobia. It must not be confused by conflicting ideas. It must not be yielded up to strange, psychic powers. At all costs, your mind must not be destroyed, because it is the seat of your will, the place where you must make all the proper decisions about how you should live and prepare yourself to meet with God at the coming of our Lord Jesus Christ.

It is an amazing thing to me that what the hypnotist seeks to do, is just what the devil has always wanted to do. The devil wishes to possess the mind of a person, to control his will. That is what he attempted to do in the Garden of Eden.

The terrible crime wave that is

engulfing the world today is certainly the result of devilish influence on the hearts and minds of men. Many times when explaining some awful deed they have done, people tell me, "A spirit told me to do it!"

The Lord Jesus wishes to be the King of our mind. Our thoughts should be about Him.

BE ON GUARD

I prophesy that in the days ahead, before Jesus Christ returns, <u>millions will have turned to every kind of spiritism</u>, including hypnotism. They will try to escape the frightening reality of life without God.

You must be on your guard. Some doctor will seek to hypnotize you or your child. Some educator may try to bring you under hypnosis to teach you something. (I hate to think what you will learn!)

In business you will have to guard against the subtle influences of salesmen who use motivating color schemes, "trigger" words, and every device imaginable in order to induce a mild form of "no-sales-resistance" hypnosis.

You may be offered a religion that soothes the conscience, smooths the rugged path of sin, and leads you into sweet forgetfulness and eternal reincarnating bliss without the Blood of Jesus Christ and ecstasy without eternal life!

I urge you never to have your fortune told. Never consult astrologers about your future or offer your mind to anyone who wishes to hypnotize you. Never attend a meeting of oriental cults, which are demon-inspired. Keep yourself clean and pure before God to walk in His ways and to serve Him.

I feel this warning, along with the warning of others, may be almost too late for the world in which we live! That is the purpose of this book, to reprove hypnotism as an unfruitful work of darkness.

Christian, this is your responsibility, too. Get this book into the hands of important people in your community, people with influence, people who might otherwise be tempted to go along with the doctors, educators, and lawyers who would make hypnotism accepted in our society. <u>If we, as enlightened Christians, do not warn the world of the danger, who will?</u>

I trust that you will understand that I am speaking the truth. I pray that you will prize your mind as a treasure from God. I beseech you not to lend your mind to someone else who might abuse it, defile it or open it up to the devil to possess.

YOUR KEY TO VICTORY

I challenge you to have the mind of Christ, a strong mind, a dedicated mind. Genesis 1:26-27 records that God created man to have dominion on earth. This dominion is achieved through your spirit and transmitted through to your mind. May you feel the power and strength of this dominion!

With Christ in your heart, no other guidance is needed. He will guide you to a happy tomorrow.

The Bible declares that our Christian

life is to be a walk of faith in which Jesus has promised to be with us every step of the way.

In these last days may the Lord Jesus Christ keep you, your spirit, soul, and body, by His mighty power.

Finally, brethren, whatsoever things are true,

Whatsoever things are honest,

Whatsoever things are just,

Whatsoever things are lovely,

Whatsoever things are of good report; if there be any virtue, and if there be any praise,

THINK ON THESE THINGS.

(Philippians 4:8)

YOU CAN KNOW
GOD'S FORGIVENESS

You need a personal Savior, a personal commitment to Him who is able and willing to forgive you of ALL your sins. Pray this Sinner's Prayer, and really mean it. He will give you peace, joy, and hope!

"Lord Jesus, I am a sinner. I believe that you died and rose from the dead to save me from my sins. Father, forgive me for yielding the control of my mind to anyone other than You. Wash me with Your blood, and I shall be clean. I ask You into my heart right now. Be my Savior and my guide forever. Amen."

In your flesh, you may not FEEL any different. But, the Word of God tells us that you are now a New Creature, and old things are passed away and forgiven. You are no longer under condemnation. You are in Christ Jesus and you now walk after the Spirit (Romans 8:1, II Corinthians 5:17, I John 2:12, Luke 7:47).

Now that you have become a child of God, please write us and we'll send you some literature to help you walk daily with the Lord. Write to: **LeSEA,** P.O. Box 12, South Bend, IN 46624. **24-hour Prayerline: (219) 291-1010.**

You can help Lester Sumrall
WIN A MILLION

God has called Lester Sumrall to win a million souls to Christ through the outreaches of the LeSEA ministry (Lester Sumrall Evangelistic Association). He showed him that the only way this would be possible is for friends and partners to work with him, pooling their resources to get the gospel out in every way possible.

When you join Brother Sumrall in this effort, you become a member of the Win-A-Million Club. Each month, you send your faithful gift of $20 or more to help with our soulwinning outreaches. . .

Christian television channels:
Channel 14-Honolulu—Channel 55-Kenosha
Channel 47-Tulsa
WHME-South Bend & WHMB-Indianapolis
WHRI-Shortwave & WHME-FM Christian radio
Missionary Assistance
World Harvest Homes
2,000 orphans in fourteen countries
World harvest Magazine
World Harvest Bible College—South Bend
24-Hour Prayerline (219) 291-1010
Christian Center School, South Bend
Video Teaching Tape Ministry—world-wide
Books, tracts, pamphlets, teaching syllabi
Campmeetings—Conferences—Crusades

As a Win-A-Million partner, you receive a beautiful gold lapel pin and the World Harvest Magazine. Simply write and say, "Here's my gift to help, I want to be a Win-A-Million partner." The Address is:

Dr. Lester Sumrall
P.O. Box 12
South Bend, Indiana 46624